Foolproof
MACHINE QUILTING

- Learn to Use Your Walking Foot
- Paper-Cut Patterns for No Marking, No Math
- Simple Stitching for Stunning Results

MARY MASHUTA

C&T PUBLISHING

Text copyright © 2008 by Mary Mashuta

Artwork copyright © 2008 by C&T Publishing, Inc.

Publisher: Amy Marson

Creative Director: Gailen Runge

Acquisitions Editor: Jan Grigsby

Editor: Liz Aneloski

Technical Editors: Carolyn Aune and Amanda Siegfried

Copyeditor/Proofreader: Wordfirm Inc.

Cover Designer/Book Designer: Kristen Yenche

Page Layout Artist: Rose Scheifer-Wright

Production Coordinators: Matt Allen and Casey Dukes

Illustrator: Kirstie L. Pettersen

Photography by Luke Mulks and Diane Pedersen of C&T Publishing unless otherwise noted

Published by C&T Publishing, Inc., P.O. Box 1456, Lafayette, CA 94549

Library of Congress Cataloging-in-Publication Data

Mashuta, Mary.

 Foolproof machine quilting : learn to use your walking foot--paper cut patterns for no marking, no math--simple stitching for stunning results / Mary Mashuta.

    p. cm.

 Includes index.

 Summary: "Learn how to machine quilt using paper-folded and cut simple shapes to create quilting designs. Techniques included for using a variety of thread weights and stitches"--Provided by publisher.

 ISBN 978-1-57120-509-4 (paper trade : alk. paper)

 1. Machine quilting. 2. Patchwork. I. Title.

 TT835.M38428 2008

Printed in China

10 9 8 7 6 5 4 3 2 1

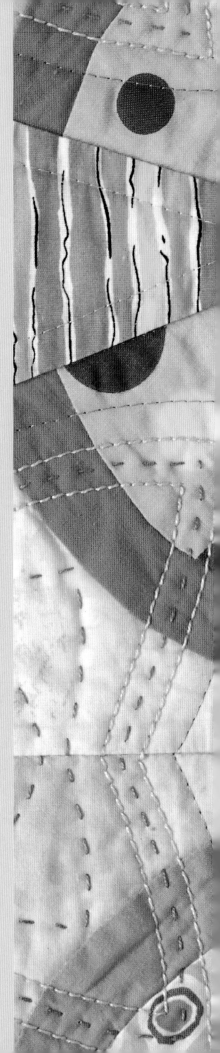

Contents

Introduction

When I began making quilts in the early 1970s, everyone I knew hand quilted. It took me almost 20 years to try machine quilting. Today many quilters begin with machine quilting.

As a professional who teaches machine quilting with the walking foot and the feed dogs up, I have worked with both beginners and those wishing to improve their skills. However, there is a lot more besides the basics to share, because I have discovered that I can create my own quilting designs that leave no telltale markings on my quilts. And, believe it or not, they are easy to stitch with a little practice.

I paper-fold and cut simple shapes or sometimes even adapt commercial templates, then transfer them to freezer paper or self-adhesive shelf paper. I place the shapes on top of the quilt, secure them in place, and stitch around them. Sometimes I add additional shapes, lines, or decorative stitching to make the designs more intricate.

As an added bonus, I have learned to sew with some of the heavier threads as the top thread on the machine, which really helps showcase my quilting designs.

This book is full of information and pictures showing what you can do with the walking foot and the feed dogs up. You may also be able to adapt some of the information to hand or free-motion quilting on your own. When I began machine quilting, I just wanted to wake up the next morning and be an expert like Harriet Hargrave, a pioneer in using an electric needle. Of course, that didn't happen. It takes practice. We all have to pay our dues, but I hope I can shorten your journey while also making it enjoyable.

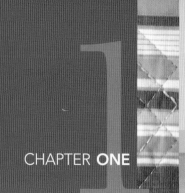

Why the Walking Foot for Quilting?

CHAPTER ONE

There is a great deal of interest in machine quilting these days, but there are many ways it can be accomplished.

WALKING-FOOT VS. FREE-MOTION QUILTING

Walking-Foot Machine Quilting

Walking-foot quilting is achieved with the feed dogs up, as in normal stitching. The walking foot pulls the top layers of the textile sandwich (quilt top, backing, and batting) through the machine as the feed dogs pull the bottom layers through, thus feeding all layers through the machine evenly. Without the walking foot, there would be "drag" lines on the quilt back.

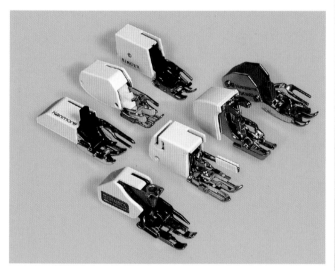

Walking feet

Traditionally, walking-foot machine quilting is most often used to stitch in the ditch close to, but not on top of, pieced seams. The stitching is a structural element that fastens the basic areas of the quilt sandwich together. The stitches only show upon close examination.

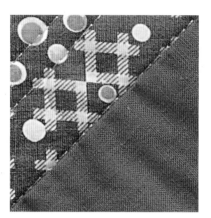

Detail of stitching in the ditch

However, walking-foot quilting can also be used to create designs that mirror or enhance the basic construction of the quilt and bring it to life.

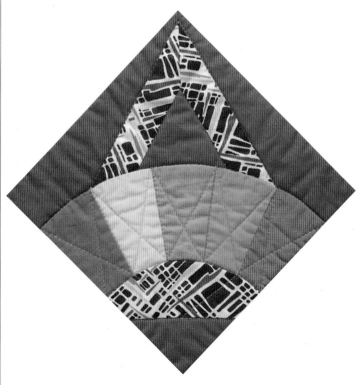

Additional straight-line stitching is added to the stitching in the ditch.

Free-Motion Machine Quilting

In free-motion quilting, on the other hand, you drop the feed dogs and move the fabric, drawing designs with the needle and thread. You control the direction and length of the stitches. Absolutely beautiful designs can be created, but the learning curve is long. As a quilt judge, my most-often-used comment regarding free-motion quilting is, "Work on the evenness of the stitch length and the smoothness of the curves."

Free-motion quilting

THE WORLD BEYOND STITCHING IN THE DITCH

In exploring walking-foot quilting, I have discovered the following:

- Accuracy can be gained by sewing at a slower, more comfortable speed, rather than at the faster speed often recommended in free-motion quilting.

- By lengthening the stitch, you can really show off the beautiful threads available today. As an added bonus, the fabric moves through the machine easier as you stitch along.

- You can use some wonderful heavier threads on the top of your machine. These threads really help showcase your quilting designs.

- If your machine has decorative stitches, it is possible to use some of them as part of your quilting designs. You paid for them, why not learn to use them?

Less Is More

Simple quilting designs can be very effective. The repetition of using a block design in 9, 16, or 25 blocks increases the quilting's impact and visually ties the quilt blocks together. This is also true of border and sashing designs.

More Is More

Walking-foot machine quilting is fun once you get past the basic in-the-ditch stitching. I often use the same block patterns again. It's an opportunity to use different fabrics *and* to try out different quilting designs.

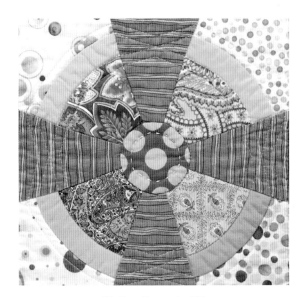

(Full quilt, page 20)
Machine stitched with 40-weight thread
Hand stitched with 30-weight thread

(Full quilt, page 55)
Machine stitched with 30- and 40-weight threads
Hand stitched with 30-weight thread

What Can You and Your Your Machine Do?

SEWING MACHINE FEATURES

You can learn to become one with your machine while machine quilting. Begin by evaluating your present equipment to determine whether it is going to be a good team player.

Buying a sewing machine is like buying a car. Some have more features or extras than do others. Here are the features I find most helpful for machine quilting with the walking foot.

Needle-Down Position

With this option, the needle stops inserted down into your fabric, making it easy to raise the foot and pivot, turn, or reposition your quilt without it shifting under the presser foot. It also makes stitching circles or curves easier.

Presser-Foot Lifter

This feature lifts the presser foot but not the needle. It allows you to reposition the fabric quickly using both hands.

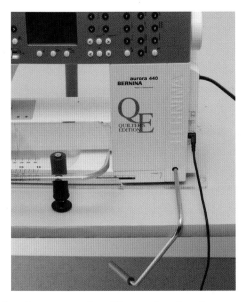

Bernina presser-foot lifter or free-hand system

If you have trouble using your right leg and foot to press on the control to run the machine and do lifts at the same time, move the foot control to your left foot to separate the "driving" and "lifting" tasks. My students adapt quickly to this adjustment. You can also rest your right foot on an ergonomic footrest to help balance your legs and hips.

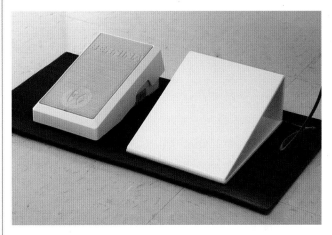

Presser foot on the left and footrest on the right

Other machines may have different ways to operate this helpful feature, so make sure to check into it.

Variable Speeds

Changing to a slower speed helps when you feel that the machine is running away with you. Some machines have a feature that slows the motor even though you're still pressing with the same force on the foot control. Free-motion teachers often encourage students to sew faster and "get into the zone," like athletes. But for walking-foot quilting, slower stitching is less stressful and more accurate.

Sewing Machine Bed

For many years, the size of the opening between the needle on the left and the machine body on the right has been about the same. But quilters wanting to machine quilt their creations have changed that. Some models now have a wider machine bed, which makes it easier to maneuver the textile sandwich through the opening while working. This is a great option.

MACHINE HEALTH

It is important to have your machine serviced according to the manufacturer's recommendations. However, routine maintenance is up to you. Remove lint, apply oil, and change your needle frequently. How often? Some say every eight hours of sewing. I say at least make sure you change the needle every time you begin quilting a new project or when you get a burr on the needle.

WALKING FOOT

For most machines, the walking foot is a separate attachment. Because all walking feet do not do an equally good job, they can either help or hinder you in reaching your goal of producing a satisfying project.

A walking foot designed specifically for your particular sewing machine is going to work best. If it's not possible to buy or order one, try a generic walking foot. Be aware, however, that generic walking feet are just like one-size-fits-all clothing. You may be lucky and find a good fit, but sometimes the results aren't perfect.

Open-Toe Foot

Closed-toe and open-toe feet for the walking foot

Many walking feet are constructed with a little piece of metal that goes across the foot in front of the needle. An open-toe foot that does not have a bar makes it easier to see where you are stitching. Sometimes you have a choice and can change the foot. Other times, however, this isn't an option, and you will have to be the one to adapt.

Seam Guide for Walking Foot

When stitching straight lines, I use masking or painter's tape as a guide and stitch next to it.

When I need to stitch narrowly spaced curved lines, I use the side edge of the walking foot as a guide. Stitching wider curves is easy with an attachable seam guide—the tip of the guide traces the curve. The curve depth can be adjusted to the width you want.

Seam guide for walking foot

Even better are seam guides for both the right and the left sides of the foot. Otherwise, you have to figure out how to mirror from only one side, and sometimes you may end up with lots of fabric stuffed onto the bed of the machine.

THE OPERATOR BEHIND THE WHEEL

Do you need new glasses? It is more difficult to see what is going on with your stitching when you are trying to focus through bi- or trifocal glasses. Many people have separate computer glasses, which may be a good option for your machine quilting. If you decide that you need glasses to magnify your work, you should determine the necessary focal length. To do so, sit comfortably at the machine and have someone measure the distance from your eyes to the needle of the machine. This is your focal length. Tell your optometrist you are a quilter and this is the focal length you would like.

TIME TO UPGRADE

You will have to be the judge of the results you get with your machine. If you decide a machine upgrade is in order, look for the features I've pointed out when you comparison shop. Local stores with good after-sales help and service are also important. It isn't necessary to purchase the top-of-the-line for this type of quilting. I have a very good midrange model from a high-end manufacturer.

YOUR QUILTING ENVIRONMENT

Most sewing machines, with their small lightbulbs, offer poor task lighting. This lighting may be adequate for daytime use, but it is usually insufficient for darker days and rooms or for evening sewing. Therefore it is a good idea to use supplemental task lighting.

Also consider your quilting chair and table. Many chairs are adjustable. A few higher-end (more costly) tables are also adjustable. These tables are great for quilters with special needs or those who aren't of average height.

Have someone take a picture of you sitting at your machine. Ideally you should sit with your elbows at a right angle and your back touching the back of your chair.

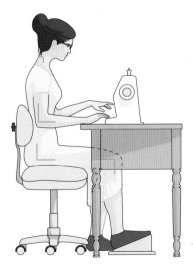

Sit at the machine with your arms in a right-angle position and your back touching the chair back for support.

If your machine isn't set into a cabinet, consider purchasing a Plexiglas surround. This additional surface expands the work surface right around your machine. Also available is a Plexiglas base that tilts your machine toward you. These can be ordered for most machines.

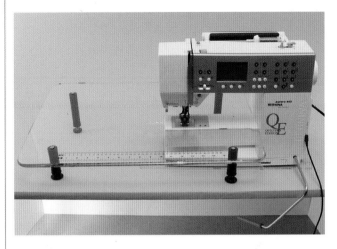

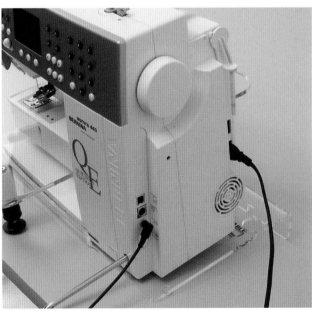

Machine with an acrylic surround that has been tilted. Some quilters say they see better and have less neck strain with this setup.

If your sewing table is small, add a TV table, card table, or adjustable ironing board to the side or back of it when quilting. The additional furniture will help support the bulk and weight of your quilt so your hands and arms don't have to do that unnecessary work.

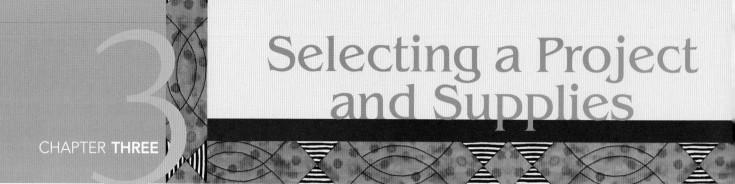

CHAPTER THREE

Selecting a Project and Supplies

It is important to pick projects carefully when you're learning walking-foot machine quilting. Small successes lead to larger successes. Overwhelming projects are discouraging and often go unfinished.

Consider the quilt's intended use. You may want to spend more time quilting your daughter's wedding quilt than you spend on the one made for your 10-year-old nephew or as a donation quilt. Competition quilts will pass under close scrutiny, so they deserve your best work.

SMALL IS BETTER

Even as an experienced quilter, I notice a big difference between working on a quilt that is 60″ × 60″ and one that is 72″ × 72″.

Consider sending large quilts to a long-arm quilter. Or your daughter might be just as happy with a wallhanging, particularly if she enjoys lying on her bed with her dogs.

You can learn a lot from using simple blocks. Larger-size blocks with fewer pieces leave more room for quilting. You can make a nice sampler quilt by adding alternate blocks, sashing, corner posts, borders, and corner blocks. Challenge yourself to come up with a different quilting pattern for each repeat block, border, and corner, as I have done in several of my quilts. Here are some simple blocks that will show off your quilting:

Nine-Patch

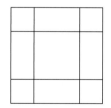
Uneven Nine-Patch

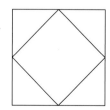
Square Within a Square

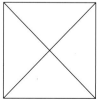
Four-Triangle Square

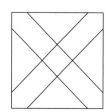
Diagonal Cross

FABRICS

Cotton fabrics give the best results, especially for beginners. Solid colors and lightly figured prints show off the quilting stitches best. It can be difficult to see the machine quilting on fabrics with busy or high-contrast prints.

THREADS

Don't put off buying the best-quality thread for your machine quilting until you are a better stitcher. Bargain thread may not give you top results. Pairing threads with the proper needles and batting also makes a big difference, so be sure you read the Needles and Batting sections (page 14).

Most machines are calibrated for 40- and 50-weight threads.

Thread sizing is confusing—the larger the number, the smaller the thread (50-weight cotton is smaller than 40-weight). I piece with 50-weight cotton, and in most cases, 50-weight is what I put in the bobbin, no matter what weight is on top of the machine.

Basic Quilting Threads

Many threads can be used for machine quilting. Just make sure you don't use hand-quilting threads, because they may be coated with an additional substance to make them stronger. Residue from this substance can build up in the eye of the machine needle.

Thicker 40-weight cotton quilting thread shows up more than 50-weight. I often use 40-weight rayons for my machine quilting, because they have more sheen than cotton has.

Polyester thread is stronger than rayon. Some experts feel that it is too strong for piecing cotton fabric but that it is fine for quilting.

Although I *could* select just one thread for my quilting, I often prefer to use several threads in one project. I may pick one thread for stitching in the ditch and outlining shapes and others for creating quilting designs that I want to show up more than basic outlining.

Some basic machine-quilting threads

40-weight cotton machine-quilting thread

40-weight rayon

30-weight Aurifil Cotton Mako 12

30-weight YLI Jeans Stitch

Poly DMC Perle Cotton #8

30-weight Aurifil Mako 12 cotton variegated

Heavier Threads

I love 30-weight threads, because the stitching really shows on the quilt surface. Quilters often place heavier weights in the bobbin, but then you have to stitch with the back of the quilt on top.

I can stitch with some 30-weight threads on the top of the machine. This only works, however, when I use specific threads with specific battings and the correct needle. (See Needles and Batting sections on page 14.)

Aurifil produces thread in many weights. Cotton Mako 12 is the heavier 30-weight one that I love.

YLI makes Jeans Stitch, a spun polyester thread that is also great for the top of the machine.

I have also used DMC Perle Cotton #8 on the top of the machine. (Even though the thread size numbering is different from the ones just mentioned, it's still the same idea; size 8 is thinner than size 5.) You will have to wind the thread onto a bobbin or empty spool, then place the new "spool" on the spindle.

YLI Polyester Jeans Stitch, Aurifil Cotton Mako 12, and DMC Perle Cotton #8

For heavier threads, I use regular 50-weight cotton in the bobbin. The top tension may need to be adjusted (dialed down to a lower number), depending on your machine.

It is imperative to bring the bobbin thread up, place both threads under the foot, and hold the two threads as you start stitching slowly. If your combination of thread, needle, and batting doesn't work on your machine, you'll find out quickly as you begin to sew.

After completing the stitching, bring the beginning and ending threads to the back and secure them. A machine's securing stitch won't work.

Hints for Working with Monofilament

1. It's imperative that there is no lint buildup under the needle in the feed dogs or in the bobbin case area. Clean it out!

2. If your machine doesn't seem to like the monofilament thread you are using, try another brand.

3. This is a delicate thread. If you place it on a vertical spindle, the thread take-up yanks at the thread as you stitch. Place monofilament thread on a horizontal spool holder or on a thread stand off the machine.

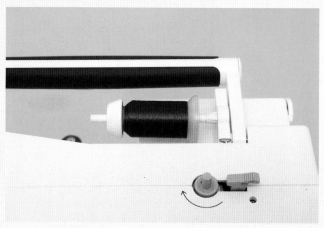

Monofilament on horizontal thread holder

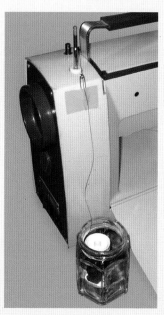

Monofilament placed in bottle and threaded through round end of safety pin thread guide

If this isn't possible, make a thread guide by taping a safety pin to the back of the machine close to the spindle, with the "circle" end up. Place the spool in a cup or bottle and thread the monofilament through the small circle in your "new" thread guide.

4. Monofilament comes in clear for lighter fabrics and smoke for darker fabrics. Stitch a sample to see which one shows the least. On black-and-white prints, it's a toss up.

5. Use a neutral-color thread in the bobbin. I use a beige or gray color. Don't worry about the color on the back of the quilt. Sometimes I use a thinner 60-weight thread, because it will show less if the bobbin loops come to the top. However, it isn't as strong as 50-weight, so make sure you have lots of other stitching on your quilt to create more stability.

6. Dialing down the top tension slightly also helps prevent the bobbin thread loop from showing on top of your work. Experiment.

7. WARNING: Don't use monofilament if you're making a baby quilt. If it comes unstitched, it could wrap around the baby's finger.

8. WARNING: Be sure to clean up stray threads if you have a cat. If kitty bathes and swallows the thread, there could be a very large vet bill.

Monofilament Thread

Monofilament thread is available in both polyester and nylon. Many quilters use it for stitching in the ditch. The good news is that the stitches don't show very much. The bad news is that it's harder to see what you're doing. If you have vision problems, don't frustrate yourself by using it.

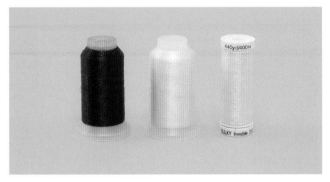

Monofilament threads

Metallic Thread

Beautiful metallic threads are a feast for the eye, but they are harder to stitch than cotton threads. Select tightly twisted, smooth metallic threads for best results while building your skills. Stay away from the flat or fuzzy threads.

Tightly twisted, smooth metallic threads are easiest to use.

When placing metallics on the machine, follow my advice in Hints 1–3 (page 12) for monofilament thread.

Variegated Threads

Several cautions are in order before you walking-foot quilt with multicolor variegated threads. Many of these threads have color changes that take a long time to occur along the length of the thread. In satin stitch or decorative motifs, the thread gets used up rapidly, but this is not the case in straight stitching. (Look carefully, however, as a few of these threads have short changes.)

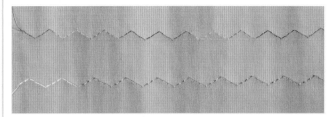

Compare short (top) and long (bottom) color changes in threads.

One-color variegated threads are more subtle, as are variegated metallics. Always stitch a sample.

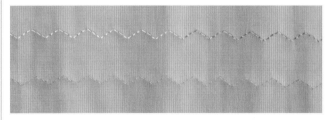

One-color variegated threads and variegated metallics are more subtle.

Select a thread that doesn't repeat the colors in your fabric, otherwise your stitching will look like it comes and goes.

Blue thread blends into blue fabric.

Select variegated threads that contrast your fabric.

There is no way to match what is happening on the top of the machine with your bobbin thread, so use a neutral thread and dial down the tension slightly to try to keep the bobbin thread from showing on the top.

NEEDLES

Believe it or not, once there was only one kind of sewing machine needle. It was called a Sharp. Now there are many. They can differ in circumference, the size and shape of the groove, how big the eye is, what the tip is like, and how the scarf on the back of the needle is shaped (the scarf helps form the loop).

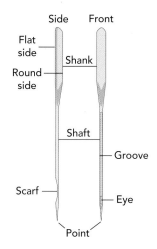

Parts of a sewing machine needle

The needle circumference is related to how thick the thread you are stitching with is. You don't want the needle holes any larger than necessary to discourage fiber migration of the batting. Finer threads need finer needles, and heavier threads need larger ones. It is easy to remember that needles are like dress sizes; the larger the number, the bigger they are.

Sharp needle tips make straighter stitching. The rounded tips on Universal needles don't pierce the fabric but slide between the threads. The only time I would use a Universal is for piecing. Some quilters don't even use a Universal then.

Size 80/12 quilting or denim needles work for medium-weight threads. Metallic threads need needles designed just for them. Look for the word *metal* in the name of the needle. When I use the heavier 30-weight threads or #8 Perle Cotton, I select a topstitching 100/16 needle. It has the biggest eye and groove and a sharp tip. Some of the thread manufacturers are now including needle information on the end of the spool. Follow their suggestions.

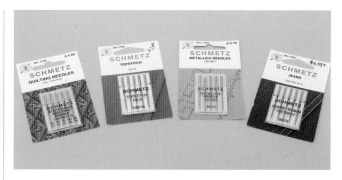

Read the needle package to select the right needle for your project.

BATTING

Many quilt battings are on the market. All are a little different, depending on how they are manufactured. Purchase quality batting, even for practicing. I am only going to discuss the three battings that I know work with the three heavier threads I just mentioned—Quilters Dream Cotton, Harriet Hargrave's Heirloom Batting for Hobbs, and Warm and Natural. Make sure you read the directions for each.

Quilters Dream Cotton is 100% cotton. It comes in different lofts, but I prefer the very thinnest (called Request) because I like the look of thin antique quilts. I also find a thin batting makes handling the textile sandwich easier as I maneuver it through the machine.

Quilters Dream Cotton doesn't have a scrim. Simply remove the batting from the package and fluff it in a cool dryer. You may need to dial more pressure on your machine presser foot when stitching, especially if you are accustomed to quilting thicker battings.

Harriet Hargrave's Heirloom Batting for Hobbs is another option. This 80% cotton/20% polyester blend has a scrim applied as part of the processing and has more loft than Quilters Dream Cotton Request. I suggest doing a presoak, as described in the directions, when using the heavier threads to slightly compress the batting and to make stitching easier.

Warm and Natural (or Warm and White) is the third option. It is also 100% cotton like Quilters Dream, but it has more loft like Harriet's batting. A good fluff in the dryer is all that is needed.

Hints for Success

I am like most quilters. I just want to start stitching and have everything work. However, as a first step, I force myself to make a sample with the thread, needle, and batting I have selected.

For every line of stitching:

- ALWAYS bring the bobbin thread up to the top of your quilt surface to avoid getting snarls on the back.
- ALWAYS hold the bobbin and top threads while you start stitching slowly.
- ALWAYS sew at a moderate, smooth speed rather than stitching with jerking stops and starts.

TROUBLESHOOTING

If you have trouble stitching, stop and try the following.

- Rethread the machine.

- Change the needle. Sometimes even new ones aren't perfect.

- If your thread is old and brittle, choose a different thread.

- If all else fails, reread the previous section and/or this chapter.

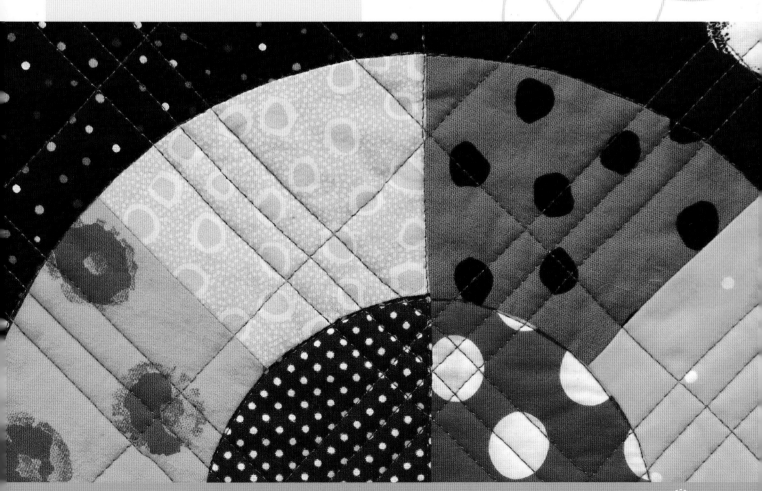

CHAPTER FOUR

Preparing the Quilt Top

When you make a good quilt sandwich, you're on the way to creating a machine-quilted project that will make you proud of yourself. Some of my students have admitted to me that they have been rather casual about these presteps. I may remind you of your high school home economics teacher, but here are some things you can grade yourself on.

PRESSING IS IMPORTANT

Press as you go while working on a project. This doesn't mean that you jump up and run to the iron for every seam sewn. You can finger-press the seams while stitching a block at the machine. Then press the completed blocks with an iron. When adding sashing, borders, or stitching blocks into rows, press them.

When deciding on the direction to press seams, try to think ahead to how you will quilt. You will have to decide a specific direction for most seams, particularly if you want to stitch in the ditch. If you press your piecing seams open, you will find it very difficult to stitch in the ditch straight, because there is no hill-and-valley pattern of bulk to follow.

Stitching in the ditch and additional quilting

On the other hand, allover designs like Baptist Fan, work best when all the seams are pressed open, because the top is flatter. Stitching in the ditch is not done with this type of allover design.

Seams pressed to one side for stitching in the ditch

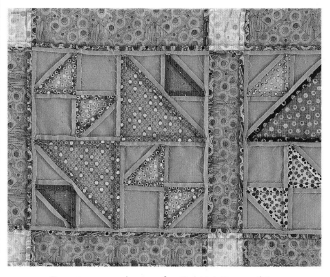

Seams pressed open for Baptist Fan quilting

Baptist Fan quilting

Preplanning is helpful. For example, your block may have a small Nine-Patch in the center, where you plan to stitch an X or a circle. The seams of the Nine-Patch part of the block could be pressed open so that they will lie flatter, even though the seams in the rest of the block are pressed in one direction to be stitched in the ditch.

A quilting plan of attack helps you be consistent while constructing and pressing the individual parts of the quilt top. If you're unable to quilt the project right away and must store the top, reinspect it when you are ready in case some seams have accidentally turned the wrong way.

SECURING EDGE SEAMS

Important: After the quilt top is finished, if there are many seams along the outside edge, machine sew a line of stitching ⅛″ from the edge around the whole quilt top. (You can lengthen the stitch slightly if it is drawing up.) If there are only large unpieced borders at the edge, stitch ½″ on either side of each seam. This important step keeps the seams from coming unstitched while you quilt.

MAKING A GOOD TEXTILE SANDWICH

Spend time getting this part right. Get a friend to help. Some quilters use the floor to pin-baste their quilts. I use a stand-up worktable because I don't "do floor" anymore. A set of inexpensive bed risers can be attached to the table legs to make them taller so you don't hurt your back. Your local quilt shop may even let you use its classroom tables.

Batting

Follow the instructions on your bag of batting. Most battings are ready to go, but it's a good idea to fluff them on your dryer's air setting for a few minutes to relax the folds. (You may actually want to presoak Harriet Hargrave's Heirloom if you want to minimize shrinkage. Read the directions. Presoaking also compresses the batting, which is helpful when quilting with heavier threads.)

Trim the batting 2″ to 4″ larger than the quilt top on all sides. If piecing is necessary, make clean cuts with a rotary cutter and butt the edges before stitching. I join the edges by hand with large catch, or herringbone, stitches that run back and forth between the two edges.

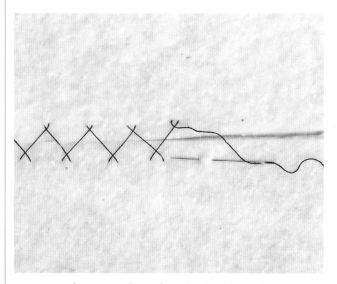

Piece batting with catch, or herringbone, stitches.

Backing

Prepare a backing fabric that is about 4″ larger than the quilt top on all sides. If seaming is necessary, press the seams open.

Place the backing fabric right-side down on the pinning surface. Hold the edges in place with small pieces of masking or painter's tape so they won't shift. Smooth the batting on top of the backing.

Quilt Top

Carefully add the quilt top. Before pinning, spend some time aligning the edges, rows, and blocks. I use both square and long rulers to make small adjustments to make sure the rows or sections are straight and the quilt top is square.

If your quilt is in good alignment before you start quilting, you will have a better chance of it being square when you finish quilting. If it's not straight now, don't expect it to look better later.

Pinning

For machine quilting, pin-baste with safety pins. There are many kinds of safety pins available. I prefer the 1⅛″ size. Smaller ones are hard to close, and larger ones often get in the way when stitching. Some quilters prefer the bent ones because they are more ergonomic to close. You can use a specific pinning tool or the side of a plastic spoon to lift the pin tip for easy closing. I have a spoon with a notch cut out of the tip that does the same thing (it is kind of like a grapefruit spoon; students tell me they have similar camping spoons). The idea is to slightly lift the closing end of the safety pin as you swoop it closed.

Pins should be placed about 4″, or a closed fist, apart. Think about where you will be stitching and avoid placing pins that will have to be removed while stitching. Pin an area and then close all the pins, assembly-line fashion. With a larger quilt, you may have to pin one section at a time.

Preparing the Edge

Add two finishing steps to the making of your textile sandwich. After all the safety pins have been placed and closed, remove the tape from the edges.

1. Working with one edge at a time, place straight pins perpendicular to the edge of the quilt about every 4″ to 5″. This allows you to even out any edge fullness.

2. Hand-baste around the edge of the quilt with needle and thread. Remove the pins as you go. Now the fabric is held at the very edge of the quilt and won't shift during stitching.

Trim the batting and backing so only a ½″ remains. This prevents the excess from accidentally getting caught under your stitching, but also leaves just a little extra in case the edge needs to be let out slightly.

Many quilters don't do these last two steps, but gladly add them after they have had problem edges.

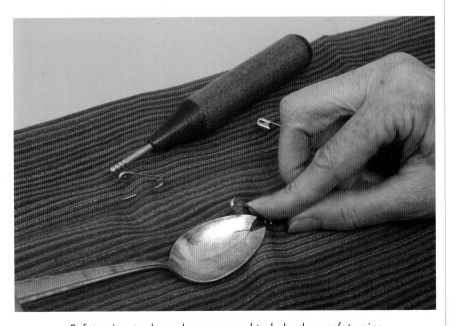

Safety pins, tools, and spoons used to help close safety pins

Creating Your Own Quilting Designs

CHAPTER FIVE

Now it's time to discover just how easy it is to create your own quilting design patterns and quilting templates for no-mark quilting.

BASIC WALKING-FOOT QUILTING

Lines have always been part of quilting. In addition to holding the quilt sandwich together, they can accent what is there structurally or in the fabric patterns. Quilted lines can also be used to provide a contrast to the quilt's pattern shapes or fabric prints.

In the previous chapter, I discussed the importance of preparing blocks during construction for the quilting that would be added later. We learned that if you want to stitch in the ditch, you press your seams to one side. If instead, you want to stitch an allover design, like the traditional Baptist Fan, that doesn't relate to block structure, you will end up with a flatter quilt if you press your seams open during construction (pages 16–17).

Just as a quick review of basic walking-foot quilting—once a quilt has been stitched in the ditch, you can add more stitching lines if you want. Although it's often not structurally necessary with the batting used today, many of us like to see more quilting lines. (Read the labeling for your batting. Many only require stitching every four or more inches.)

Look at how I quilted these simple blocks beyond the basic stitching in the ditch. I either used the edge of the walking foot as a guide or stitched along masking or painter's tape placed from point to point to ensure that my stitching was straight. I did not do any marking on the quilts.

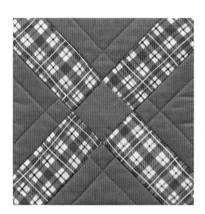

(Full quilt, page 20)
Straight stitching (marked with ¾˝ tape)

(Full quilt, page 20)
Straight stitching (marked with ¾˝ tape) + X in center

(Full quilt, page 20)
Stitched in the ditch across square and continued across triangle (marked with tape)

Cross and Nine-Patch

Reproduction Eight-Pointed Star Quilt

Sassy Baskets

Trumpet Vine

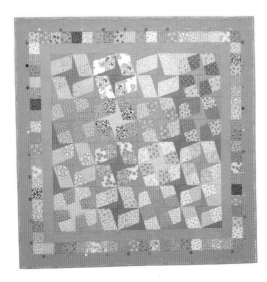

Fiesta Stars

Paisley Propellers

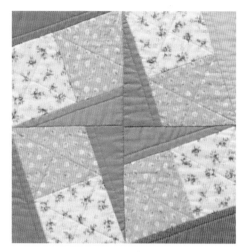

(Full quilt, page 20)
Straight stitching for star points
(using edge of walking foot)
+ all other lines (marked with tape)

(Full quilt, page 20)
Star outline stitched (marked with ¾″ tape)

Straight stitching (using edge of walking foot)
Curves (stitching in the ditch)

COMMERCIAL TEMPLATES

Now it's time to go beyond the basics to look at other possibilities for walking-foot machine quilting.

Many commercially made stencil templates are available. They are intended, however, for hand quilting or free-motion continuous-line machine quilting, in which a chalk or lead pencil is used to trace through the stencil cutouts to transfer the design to the quilt.

I won't draw on my quilts or garments, since I've had several less-than-satisfactory experiences in removing the markings. However, I can still use stencil designs if they are made of shapes that can be cut apart and used separately after being transferred to freezer or self-adhesive shelf paper. When looking at the different stencils available, I ask myself, "Are the designs simple to stitch around?" and "How large are the component pieces?"

Commercially cut acrylic and plastic template shapes are also on the market. Several sizes are nested in a set (page 22), but only the largest work for my type of quilting. Since these are more expensive than quilting design stencils, I have to decide how badly I want the shape.

I began my walking-foot machine quilting by relying on the commercial stencils that I had purchased for my quilting patterns. Looking back, I realize that I could have cut many of the shapes on my own. Although I now know how to change the size and placement of the individual units, I still look at what is available commercially, because sometimes I find shapes I would not be able to cut on my own. For example, a five-pointed star or a Baptist Fan template would be hard for me to figure out, so they are worth every penny.

Commercial stencils

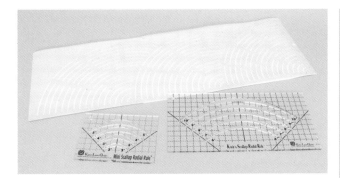

Baptist Fan stencil and scallop templates

OTHER QUILTING PATTERN POSSIBILITIES

You may have other possibilities for quilting design shapes lying around your house—just look. If you don't have a compass to draw a circle, try tracing around teacups, saucers, jar lids, and CDs. Newspapers, magazines, simple children's books, and your junk mail are all potential sources of simple shape ideas. I was even able to trace the shape of a large refrigerator magnet and turn it into a wonderful flower quilting design.

Handy shapes around the house to use in creating quilting patterns

Templates or refrigerator magnet to use as flower shapes

PAPER-CUTTING YOUR OWN TEMPLATES

You can paper-cut to create simple shapes when making your own templates. No drawing is necessary.

Simple Folded Shapes

When we were children, many of us folded paper and cut snowflakes, even if we lived where snow never fell.

The basic steps for cutting snowflakes apply to cutting the much simpler shapes needed for machine-quilting design templates. Many of the template shapes involve even fewer folds than the snowflakes.

In paper cutting, if you don't succeed on your first try, you can adapt your shape by refolding the paper and snipping a little off here or there. If slight changes don't help, you can throw it away and start again. On the next try, you have a better idea of what to do.

Cut a square of paper.   Fold 1: Fold the square of paper in half into a rectangle.

Fold 2: Fold in half again.

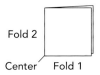

Fold 3: Hold the center with your thumb and pointer finger. Fold the top section of the square diagonally to the front.

Fold 4: Fold the remaining section diagonally to the back.

Simple Folded Quilting Designs

Remember, you are cutting simple shapes, or silhouettes, to outline with stitching. Keep telling yourself that *less is more*. The more nooks and crannies you have, the more you have to stop and pivot.

Straight lines and soft curves are easier to stitch than lots of pivots. However, points at the edge of a petal shape may be easier to stitch than having to execute a small curve at the tip in two smooth stitches.

Simple shapes are the basis of quilting designs.

Fold the square in eighths as shown on page 22, *rotate* the folded triangular piece so the folds are in the location shown, then cut on the red lines. You will have a perfectly symmetrical shape to use as a design.

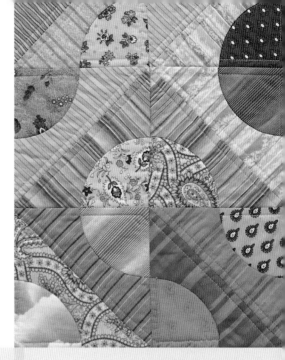

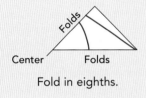

Fold in eighths.

Cut.

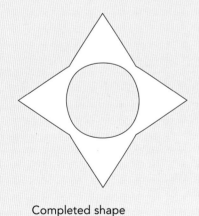

Completed shape

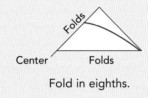

Fold in eighths.

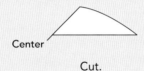

Center

Cut.

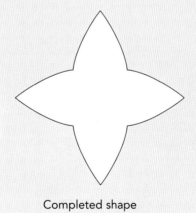

Completed shape

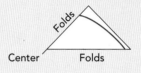

Fold in eighths.

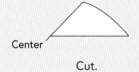

Center

Cut.

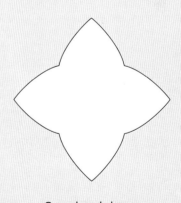

Completed shape

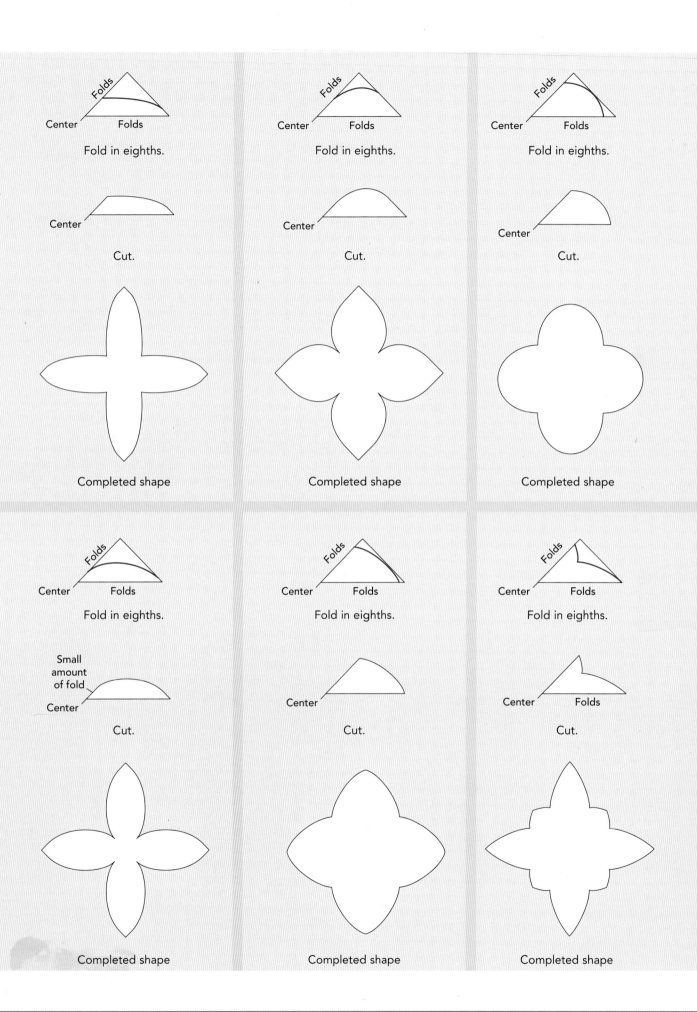

Folds

Center · Folds

Fold in eighths.

Center

Cut.

Completed shape

Folds

Center · Folds

Fold in eighths.

Center

Cut.

Completed shape

Folds

Center · Folds

Fold in eighths.

Center

Cut.

Completed shape

Folds

Center · Folds

Fold in eighths.

Small amount of fold

Center

Cut.

Completed shape

Folds

Center · Folds

Fold in eighths.

Center

Cut.

Completed shape

Folds

Center · Folds

Fold in eighths.

Center · Folds

Cut.

Completed shape

Keep in Mind

- Size makes a difference. Large circles are easier to stitch smoothly than are small ones. I sometimes shorten my stitch length slightly for curves if they aren't looking smooth.

- How many times will a design need to be repeated in a quilt? For a quilt with 9 repeat blocks, you will have to stitch your design 9 times; if there are 25 blocks, 25 times.

- For more complex designs, multiply the difficulty and length of time by the number of blocks to be stitched to decide whether you want to get more elaborate.

- You could also decide to stitch more complex designs only in corner blocks. Because they are at the edge of the quilt, they would only have to be repeated four times.

MAKING THE TEMPLATES

You may be surprised how few quilting templates you will actually have to cut once you have worked out your design.

When you're quilting a repeat block quilt, one set of templates is probably adequate for the whole quilt. If you are doing a repeat border design, you will cut enough shapes to fill the length of one side and then reuse them for the other sides.

Transfer your paper or commercial designs to freezer or self-adhesive shelf paper (Contac paper). Simply trace the shape(s) with a pencil and cut. (It may take several strokes of the pencil to make a dark enough cutting line.)

Freezer paper is a little sturdier than regular paper. The shiny side of the paper will adhere to your quilt if you iron it in place with the dull side up. Or you can pin the shapes in place. Borders usually need to be pinned because several pieces are required.

I use self-adhesive shelf paper because it is sturdier than freezer paper and comes in colors other than plain white. You want good contrast with your quilt fabrics, so make sure you don't buy Contac paper that has a busy print or the one that is clear. (Warning: Do not press self-adhesive shelf paper with your iron.)

It's much easier to transfer your designs onto self-adhesive shelf paper that has a paper backing. (Hint: Peek inside the end of the tube if it's prepackaged to see if it has a backing.) The gridded backing is easy to draw on and is removed after cutting. Sometimes self-adhesive shelf paper with backing can be purchased by the foot from a roll. Buy several colors. If your first choice doesn't contrast as well as you thought it would, you have a backup.

If you can't find self-adhesive shelf paper with a paper backing, unroll the paper and smooth it on your table while you transfer the design.

CHAPTER SIX

Let's Quilt!

FINDING SOLUTIONS

Before the fun begins, here are some answers to questions that might come up.

QUESTION: What about stitching in the ditch first?

I stitch in the ditch before I add the decorative stitching. You will have to decide how much stitching is enough for your quilt.

QUESTION: What weight thread should I use?

I use 40-weight rayon for stitching in the ditch and for some of the decorative stitching. (Some quilters prefer cotton or polyester thread.)

The motifs shown in this book were stitched in heavier threads:

> Aurifil Mako 12: 30-weight cotton
> YLI Jeans Stitch: 30-weight polyester
> DMC Perle Cotton: #8 (comparable to 30-weight)

QUESTION: How many starts and stops will there be on a motif?

It's nice to have just one start and stop to outline a motif. However, it's often easier to stitch one half of the design and then the other half.

Be realistic about the quilt's size and bulk and how easy it is to pivot the quilt on the bed of the machine.

Multiple motifs can be prettier, but they add stitching and knotting time. It's easiest to stitch complicated designs at the edges of the quilt.

Except for some straight lines, the decorative stitching and silhouette motifs will need to have the threads brought to the back, knotted, and the knots worked in just like hand quilting (page 28).

Start and stop your stitching on inside points, where it is easiest to manipulate joining the beginning and ending stitches. It's a lot harder to match up stitching on outside curves and on points of motifs, where inaccuracies really show.

QUESTION: How do I deal with the bulk of the quilt?

To help support the quilt, add a TV table, card table, and/or adjustable ironing board to the side and back of the machine. For larger quilts, roll up the edge of the quilt that goes under the arm of the machine when grid quilting. After this step, you can open out the quilt and just bring up smaller portions to work on. Let the table(s) support the bulk of the quilt.

QUESTION: What if the design doesn't show as much as I'd like it to?

▪ Use thread with more contrast, such as a lighter or darker value. Or switch thread color entirely so it contrasts more with the fabric print.

(Full quilt, page 57)
Quilted motifs on green background stitched with green thread

(Full quilt, page 57)
Quilted motifs on green background quilted with contrasting pink thread

- Stitch around a motif a second time, ⅛″ away from the design, to make it bolder.

The flower is more visible with a second mirroring line of stitching.

- Change the size of the thread to a heavier weight.

Decorative stitching in blocks quilted with 40-weight thread

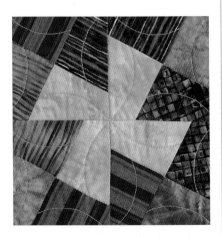

Decorative stitching in blocks quilted with DMC Perle Cotton #8

QUESTION: What if my design is too small for the area?

- Recut the motif.

- Add a second line of mirroring stitching around the motif, using the edge of the walking foot as a guide.

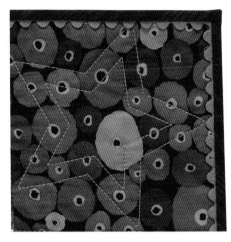

(Full quilt, page 42)
A second line of stitching makes the star bigger, but it's also easier to see on this busy print.

QUESTION: How can I make a motif more interesting?

Add hand quilting and embellishments to the quilted motifs.

The corner block has three superimposed motifs stitched in 30-weight thread. The space is nicely filled.

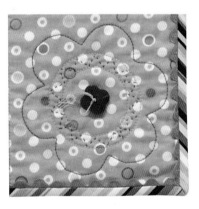

(Full quilt, page 61)
Hand stitching and button embellishment added to the corner motif

QUESTION: What if I stick myself and get blood on my quilt?

Try to make sure that the long ends of the pins are tucked back into the quilt, so they are less likely to get caught in the walking foot or to stick you. If you do get blood on the quilt, wad up a length of white thread, place it in your mouth, and get it really wet with saliva. Dab the spot with the thread before the spot has a chance to dry. Only your saliva will work on your blood.

OPTIONS FOR SECURING THE STITCHES

Because you don't want your quilting to come out, you'll have to decide how to start and stop. Many machines have a securing stitch, which goes up and down in place three times, but this is insufficient for our purposes.

For straight stitching with regular-weight threads, it is possible to stitch very small stitches for $1/8''$–$1/4''$ to begin and end the stitching. Experiment. If you get a clump, you have dialed too small. If the stitches pull out, dial smaller stitches or stitch more of them.

On most machines, you have to dial the small stitches, sew a short distance, stop, redial to a longer stitch length for your line of straight stitching, and then change back to the small stitches at the end of your line of stitching. My students are willing to do this because the stops and starts are fairly inconspicuous.

Stitch very small stitches to start and stop.

Another option is to use a small zigzag stitch method that Californian Helen White taught me. However, to do so, you will need a machine that stitches a zigzag width of less than 0.5 mm (most don't). I dial down the width and the length and do five to seven swings of the needle. You can hardly even tell it's a zigzag.

Small zigzag starting and stopping stitches

On my computerized machine, I can have two stitches active at the same time. I am able to toggle back and forth between my stop/start zigzag stitching and the longer-length stitches that I have set for straight stitching. (This doesn't work for decorative stitch patterns, however, because of preset needle positions.)

For serious competition quilts, you may have to bring the threads to the back and knot and tie them off as in hand quilting. After tying the knot, thread a needle with the thread tails and pull the knot through the fabric so it is lodged between the layers. Trim the excess tails. You will also have to do this if you use some of the heavier threads. (Monofilaments and metallic will need to be secured on the top side with tiny machine stitches because they can't be tied off easily.)

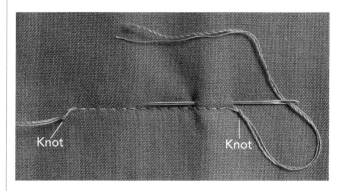

Secure quilting stitches by hand

MACHINE ADJUSTMENTS

Depending on the machine and the thread type and size, you may have to change the tension of the top thread. If your bobbin thread doesn't match your top thread or if you are using monofilament, metallic, or heavier threads, try a slightly lower number top tension, so the top thread is pulled just slightly to the back of the quilt. If possible, I match my top and bottom threads in color. Heavy thread on top doesn't need heavy on the bottom; it may just need a tension adjustment.

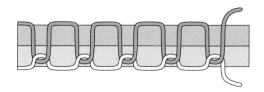

Adjust tension

Sometimes you can get better stitch quality by applying more pressure to the walking foot so the fabric is held more firmly. I find this helpful when using a wider-bodied walking foot—such as the kind that comes with some newer sewing machines—to quilt the very thin batting I prefer (page 17).

STITCHING IN THE DITCH

This basic stitching is done as structural stitching to hold the quilt sandwich parts together before adding more decorative stitching. Stitching in the ditch helps make the quilt flat. You will have to determine how much stitching is enough for your project.

For this stitching, you can use monofilament, rayon, cotton or polyester thread. I use rayon because it's easier for me to see and has a nice sheen.

Stitching in the ditch is done very close to seams that were pressed to one side during construction. The idea is to stitch on the side of the seam with the least bulk. (If you stitch on top of the bulky side, it will show just as topstitching does on a shirt collar.) Pay attention when doing this stitching because the bulky side can switch sides at seam intersections.

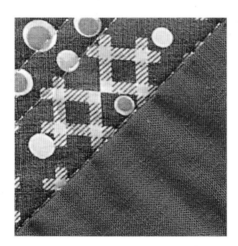

Stitching in the ditch

As an example, for a sashed block quilt, I always stitch at least a basic grid that outlines both sides of the sashing. I begin by stitching a "cross," with one vertical row and then one horizontal row as near to the middle of the quilt as the sashing seams allow. I roll the quilt vertically and then horizontally and feed it through the machine. I always stitch ¼" of small securing stitches (page 28) at the very edge because some might get cut off when I true up the quilt.

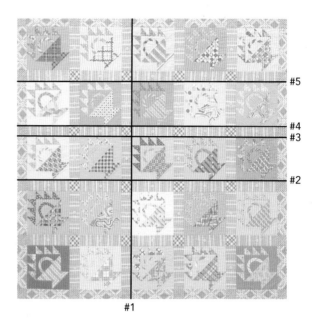

Order for stitching in the ditch of a sashed quilt

After stitching the remaining grid, I open the quilt and remove any safety pins that are no longer needed, such as those in the sashing. I then decide how much more stitching in the ditch to do. Since the quilt is held together by this structural stitching and by the hand stitching at the edge, I can work on any part of the quilt that suits me. This has a real advantage over hand quilting, which requires working from the "belly button" out.

I begin machine quilting on the blocks nearest the edge or the quilt border. This is a good time to build your skill before working in the center of the quilt, where you will have to deal with more fabric bulk.

BASIC SEWING TIPS

If you are stitching a flower or circle, the threads will definitely have to be brought to the back and tied off, because starting and stopping stitches would be too obvious.

It is important to make sure that your machine needle is always in the down position when you pivot or make a slight correction in stitching a curved line. If you are lucky, your machine will have a needle-down position, which makes this easier to do.

What do you do if a stitch doesn't go exactly where you had planned? With some machines, you can actually remove the very last stitch taken if you are sewing slowly and realize that the needle went into the wrong place. With others, once a stitch is stitched, that is it! In that case, you will have to decide whether to leave the "error" stitching or take it out. In either case, sewing slowly is helpful in critical stitching areas. (If I have to take stitching out, I carefully remove it just far enough back to hide a new ending and a new beginning, for example, at a seam or intersection.)

DECORATIVE STITCHES

Many quilters have never used the decorative stitches on their machine, and yet some stitches adapt very well to machine quilting. Experiment with changing the stitch length and/or width. This is often necessary when using heavier threads.

As we shall see, a great deal can be done with decorative stitches.

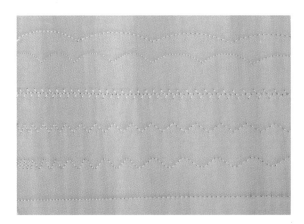

Changing a decorative stitch from the default setting to a longer length

POSITIONING AND STITCHING AROUND TEMPLATES

I use long daisy pins to secure my shapes in place. This way, if I sew over the pins, the walking foot will glide over the flat daisy heads. The foot will always get caught on glass-headed pins. In either case, just be careful not to stick yourself.

If you're going to stitch one block at a time and your machine has a surround area, stay at the machine and just do the pinning in front of you block by block.

Take time to center the template shape within the block. If there are multiple shapes, concentrate on just one at a time as you build the design. Start with the largest template and work in toward the center. Then you can see what you've already stitched.

Complex quilting design: One shape has been stitched.
The second shape is pinned with daisy pins.

Complex quilting design:
Two shapes have already been stitched.

When stitching circular motifs made of segments, the basic stitching pattern is repeated from segment to segment in what looks like a continuous line of stitching. It is easiest to cut and pin individual templates for half the design, stitch, and then repeat for the second half of the block. The individual templates give you flexibility while stitching and also allow for any piecing irregularities. However, as you will notice in the photograph, the thin circular shape outlining the half-circle was cut in one continuous piece for ease of handling. In this case, individual pieces would be too small.

Four repeat shapes are pinned and ready for stitching. The other half of the block has already been stitched.

A pleasing shape is cut.

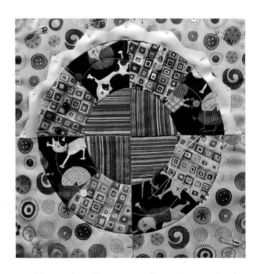

Additional quilting is ready to be stitched.

Using Border Templates

When you quilt a continuous border design made from repeating shapes, you will need to cut enough templates for one border. Pin the templates and stitch. Repeat for the remaining borders.

When you're ready to position the border templates, lay the quilt on the ironing board or on a worktable. Place the middle element first and work out toward the two ends. Leave small spaces to stitch between the connecting shapes.

Three repeat shapes are needed to stitch half the block.

If you're using freezer paper instead of self-adhesive shelf paper, you can "kiss" the shapes with the iron as you place them. You can also add pins to make sure they stay securely in place. Borders require repeated trips to the ironing board to position the templates on each border. You will be getting up and down a lot, but it is good to change your position between steps to lessen tension buildup in your muscles.

Stitch next to the pinned templates.

Enough repeats are cut to stitch the entire border length and are then pinned in place.

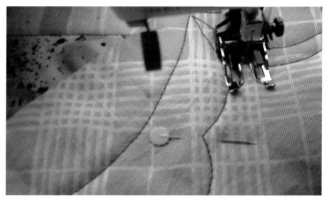

A second line of stitching is added using the edge of the foot as a width guide. A daisy pin denotes where to pivot.

Tips: Sewing Around Templates

- Be sure you make a sample for stitch length and compatibility of thread, needle, and batting. Experiment using about eight stitches per inch (3–4.0 mm).

- Position the portion of the quilt you will be stitching on the bed of the machine. Make sure you aren't supporting the weight of the rest of the quilt with your hands and arms. Auxiliary tables and ironing boards may help.

- Bring up the bobbin thread. Place it and the top thread underneath the foot. Hold the two threads as you begin slowly stitching the first couple of stitches.

- Sew at a slow-to-moderate speed. (You may be able to change to a slower speed on your machine.)

- Use the needle-down position if available. Otherwise, keep telling yourself to be aware of where the needle is when you stop stitching and want to pivot.

- When pivoting the quilt, use the hands-free mechanism if your machine has it. You'll find it makes changing the position of the foot much easier and faster.

- It's often not possible to sew all the way around a block template because you can turn or twist the quilt bulk only so far. Plan to stitch halfway around the template, stop the stitching, reposition, and then sew the other half. This means you will bring up the bobbin thread twice to start. There are more starts, stops, and knotting in walking-foot machine quilting than with free-motion quilting.

- When stitching border designs, try for long, curving lines rather than lots of pivots. A continuous border design will have only one set of starts and stops for each line of stitching.

- Make sure to leave a length of thread when you stop stitching. Most often, threads will have to be brought to the back, knotted, and worked in. (Sometimes you can use small securing stitches with 40-weight threads, but securing stitches cannot be used with heavier 30-weight threads.)

- Carefully remove the pins and template. If your stitching has caught slightly in the template, hold the stitched area as you gently pull the template away.

POSSIBILITIES

In addition to making serious quilts, I've made lots of teaching samples for my classes. My students enjoy multiple examples that show different fabrics. An added bonus for making these samples is that I can try out different quilting solutions.

Even if you don't make multiple same-block quilts, you can turn one quilt into a sampler and challenge yourself to create different designs for each block and border. Four or nine blocks, sashing, four corner blocks, and four borders can give your creative mind a real workout.

Quilters are visual, and I know some of you will only look at the pictures. For those of you who can't figure out what is happening just from the picture, I've added captions that explain the process.

CONTINUOUS QUILTING DESIGNS

It is sometimes possible to come up with designs that can actually go from block to block or from one sashing section to the next.

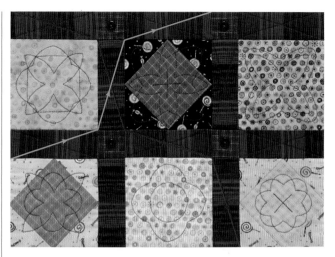

(Full quilt, page 36)
Sashing is stitched in a continuous line from one sashing segment to the next.
30-weight thread

The idea of continuous stitching can also work very well on border designs. Although there can be lots of starts and stops in walking-foot quilting, use continuous stitching whenever you can. You may not be able to stitch as far as the two examples pictured, but every line that can be continued does save time.

PIECED QUILT BLOCKS

There are four ways to create a quilting design for a pieced block. All the designs are transferred to freezer paper or self-adhesive shelf paper, secured to the quilt, and stitched.

1. If your block can be stitched with one design motif, cut a square of paper the finished block size, fold it, and cut a design.

2. If your block has a large area you want to feature (such as a center square), cut a square of paper the finished size of the area, fold it, and cut a design.

3. For a finished quilt, photocopy the desired area. Cut out, fold, and cut the design.

4. Audition already-existing template shapes by placing some of them on the quilt for inspiration.

Blocks and border triangles can be stitched in a continuing line of scallops.
40-weight thread

7˝ Pizza Block

Sometimes less is more. The Pizza block is an example of adding a simple quilted design motif to enhance the large triangle.

Triangle created by connecting midpoints
of pieced triangle sides (marked with tape)

30-weight thread

Floral Pizza

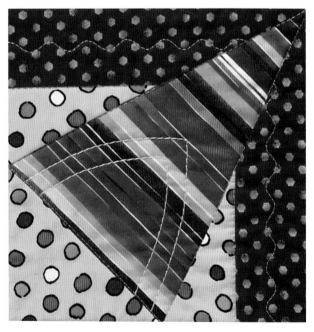

Triangle (paper-folded and cut)
Mirror stitching using edge of walking foot

30-weight thread

Stripe Pizza

6″ Square Within a Square

Four triangles and a square make up this simple pieced block. To quilt it, I used one four-petal flower shape (paper-folded and cut) and occasional straight stitching or a circle. The number of starts, stops, and knots varies, depending on whether you can completely turn the block in the machine or if you have to stop and adjust it in the machine to stitch the second half of the motif. All were stitched with 30-weight thread.

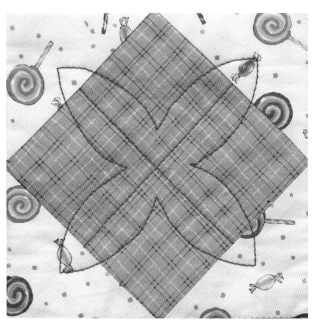

Flower + X (marked with tape)

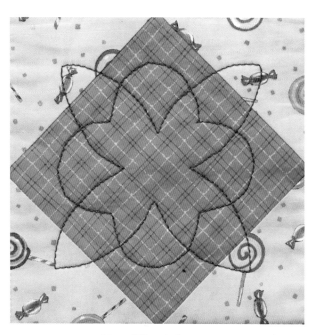

Two different flowers

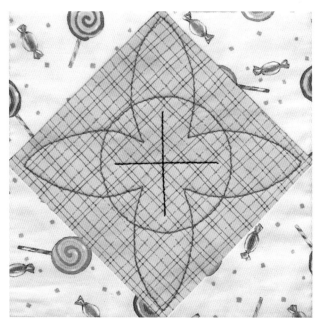

Flower + circle + X
(marked with tape)

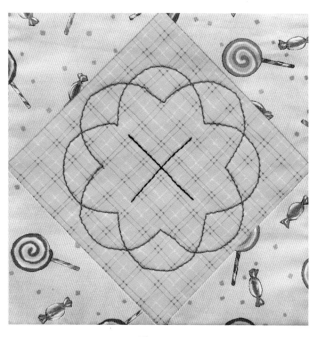

Flowers
(same template used twice) + X
(marked with tape)

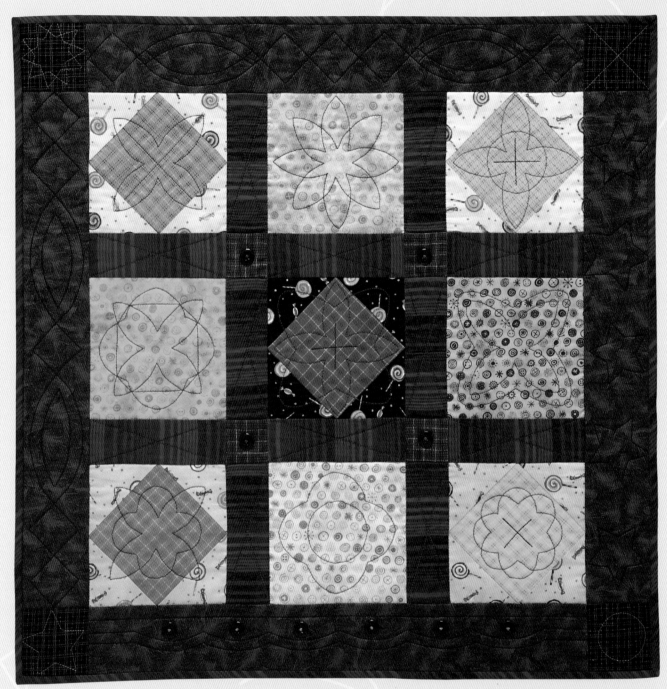

Sampler Quilt

7½″ Nine-Patch

The challenge for this quilt was to come up with as many different designs as possible. I used two flower templates (paper-folded and cut) but changed the template orientation and the number of templates used. Some blocks had mirror stitching. All were stitched with 30-weight thread.

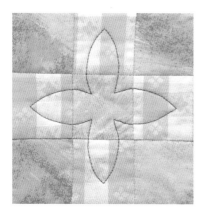

Flower
(template placed vertically)

Flower
(template placed diagonally)

Flowers
(the same template used twice—one placed vertically and one diagonally)

Flowers
Mirror stitching
(using edge of walking foot)

Flower

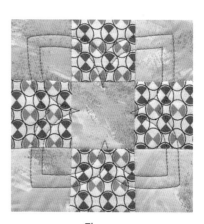

Flower
Mirror stitching
(using edge of walking foot)

Two different flowers

Flowers
(the same template used twice—one placed vertically and one diagonally; mirror stitching using edge of walking foot)

Adrian's Challenge

7½″ Diagonal Cross

The alternate block used in *Adrian's Challenge* was a Diagonal Cross. As with the Nine-Patch, I used flower templates (paper-folded and cut) and 30-weight thread.

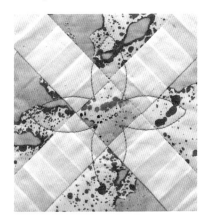

Flower
(template placed vertically)

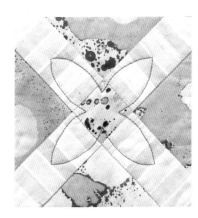

Flower
(template placed diagonally)

Flowers
(the same template used twice—one placed vertically and one diagonally)

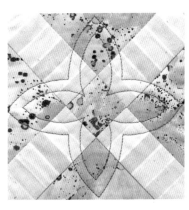

Flower
Mirror stitching

Flower

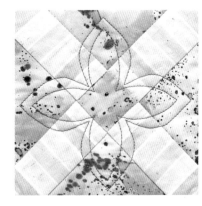

Flowers
(two templates, one inside the other)
(template placed vertically)

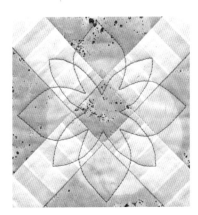

Flowers
(with two templates—one placed vertically and one diagonally)

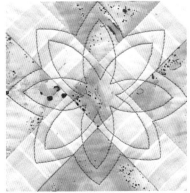

Flowers
(same template used twice around outside edge)

Mirror stitching
(using edge of walking foot)

Adrian's Challenge

12˝ Circle Within Circle

This centered-circle square block is one of my favorites because I get to make lots of fabric choices. Traditionally, eight wedges make up the circle part of the block, but I have halved or quartered the block for more contemporary variations. The block can be pieced or appliquéd.

Comparing a variety of quilting choices is once again helpful. You can always use a basic straight-line approach.

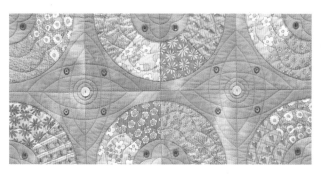

Flower (paper-folded and cut) + circle
Swag (2-sided scallop) + flower (both paper-folded and cut)
Elliptical shape (leftover Baptist Fan arcs) + circles
Buttons
30-weight thread

Straight stitching (marked with tape)
40-weight thread

However, you could also cut a curved motif from the wedge. In that case, you will only need four repeats to stitch halfway around the circle. It's better to have separate, rather than connecting, templates for the wedges so that you can fudge it if some of your wedges are a little off (page 31).

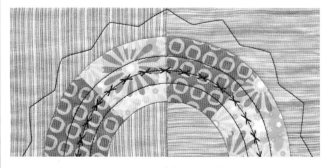

Zigzag (paper-folded and cut)
Curve made with straight stitches
(using attachable seam guide) + decorative stitches
30-weight thread

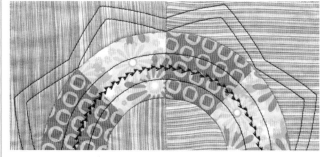

Zigzag (paper-folded and cut) + mirror stitching
30-weight thread

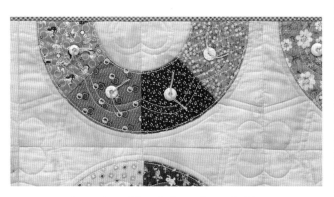

Curved motif in circle scallop stitching
(paper-fold and cut one segment)
Mirror stitching (using edge of walking foot)
Vintage buttons
30-weight thread

> **tip**
> - If you don't have an attachable seam guide, photocopy the block. Then mark 1˝ increments around the circle and connect the dots. Make a template to pin on your blocks.
>
> - The curved designs also work for three-quarter circles but not for whole ones because it would be impossible to match up the beginning and ending of the decorative stitch pattern.

Simple Baskets

I love basket blocks and have made quite a few quilts using them. The idea of parallel lines with decorative stitching added can be adapted to both straight and curved baskets.

Straight lines (marked with tape) + decorative stitch
30-weight thread

Curved lines (using attachable seam guide)
+ decorative stitch
30-weight thread

Allover Designs for Baskets

I had a quilting breakthrough when I realized that I could use the lines from the traditional Baptist Fan arcs to quilt selected areas in a quilt, rather than stitching the whole quilt as the design was intended to be used. Because I had tried this on a border (pages 20 and 61) it dawned on me that it would also work for large, pieced basket blocks.

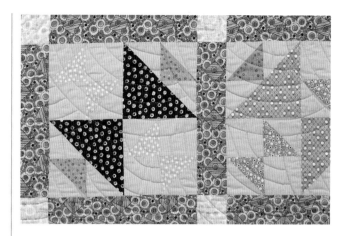

25 Binney Baskets

Lay the Baptist Fan stencil on a square of self-adhesive shelf paper the size of the block and trace the arcs you want. Cut the templates apart and pin them in place, one by one, as you stitch.

When I first tried this, I debated whether to stitch the 25 blocks in five (125 total) or six (150 total) arcs. I went with five arcs because it would take a lot less time to stitch. Unfortunately, however, after I had stitched a number of the blocks, I decided I didn't like the results. So I ended up adding a second mirroring line to each arc. Thus, by opting to save time and stitch 125 rather than 150 arcs, I actually got to stitch 250!

Well, live and learn. I could have stitched two sample blocks (but there weren't any leftovers) or made photocopies to experiment with (this latter idea hadn't dawned on me yet). It's so hard to think outside the box. This tedious lesson did teach me that there is a lot more that can be done with the traditional Baptist Fan quilting pattern.

Flowers (paper-folded and cut)
30-weight thread

5 arcs (commercial template)
Mirror stitching (using edge of walking foot)
40-weight thread

Alternate Blocks

Many block quilts have areas where unpieced fabric is alternated with the blocks. These plain blocks are a huge time-saver because fewer pieced or appliquéd blocks are needed.

Alternate Plain-Square Blocks

If your quilt blocks are placed on-square, rather than on-point, placement of motifs is easy. All the motifs will be exactly alike and fit in the same size squares.

Motifs can be stitched in many ways. Consider the size of the space to be filled, how busy your unpieced fabric is, and the color and weight of your thread. Many of the motifs we have previously seen in this chapter would work.

Stitched On-Point Alternate Blocks

Quilts that have the blocks placed on-point create more of a challenge since there are triangles, or partial blocks, at the edge of the quilt.

If you want a fast way to fill the side and corner triangles, use simple straight-line stitching. Vary the distance between the stitching lines to add more interest.

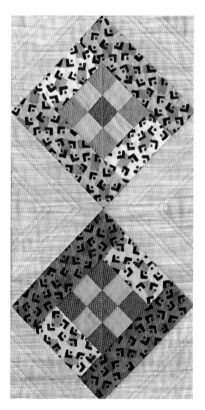

Side and corner triangles stitched using alternating line
(marked with $3/4''$ tape) + narrow lines
(using edge of walking foot)
Pivot and direction change on side triangle
40-weight thread

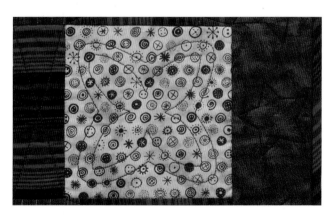

Flower (paper-folded and cut)
Mirror stitching (using edge of walking foot)
30-weight thread

Motifs for On-Point Alternate Blocks

Quilting fancier designs takes longer than quilting straight lines, but it adds much more viewer interest. Selecting a motif to place in alternate squares that can be divided in half (for side triangles) and in quarters (for corner triangles) requires thought.

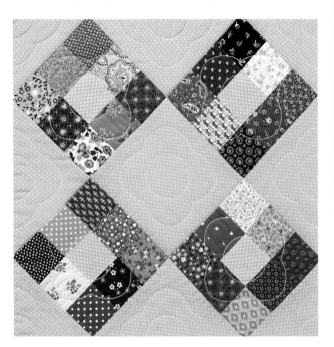

Flower (paper-folded and cut) + circle
30-weight thread

This next motif is much more difficult to stitch because of the narrow, deep spokes. It should have been rotated one degree when placing it so the half and quarter units would be more attractive. I didn't think ahead.

Hollice Turnbow stencil + circle + straight lines stitched next to seamlines (using the edge of the walking foot)
40-weight thread

I used three motifs for this example. The space is filled nicely, and the half and quarter motifs work well.

Flower (paper-folded and cut) + four-pointed star (paper-folded and cut) + circle
Mirror stitching using edge of walking foot
30-weight thread

Flower Power

Other Negative Space

Some quilts have pieces of fabric added that aren't sashing, outer borders, or alternate blocks. Instead they serve as spaces between elements, or they may be used to adjust the total size of joined elements. These areas can introduce contrasting colors, interesting fabrics, embellishments, and quilting that add to the overall enjoyment of the quilt.

In *Fix It 'Til It's Right*, vertical strips embellished with jumbo rickrack set off the whole quilt and tie the three stacks of blocks together.

I combined the vintage work of seven unknown quilters to make *Bits and Pieces*. Fabric spacers both divide and set off the disparate parts.

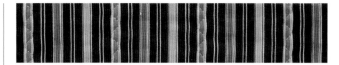

Decorative stitching
30-weight thread

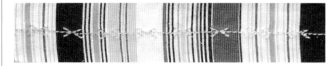

Decorative stitching
30-weight thread

Straight stitching (30-weight thread)
+ decorative stitching (40-weight thread)

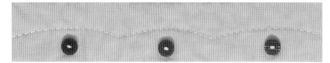

Decorative stitching
Buttons
30-weight thread

Decorative stitching (40-weight thread)
+ hand stitching (30-weight thread)

Straight stitching (40-weight thread)
+ jumbo rickrack hand stitched with
variegated Sashiko thread (30-weight)

Fix It 'Til It's Right

Bits and Pieces

Sashing

Blocks are often joined with sashing. I consider sashing with corner posts to be my "default" setting when I design a quilt. Structurally, stitching in the ditch is usually enough, but the fun has really just begun.

The quickest way to make sashing more interesting is to add decorative stitches down the center of all the pieces. But diagonal straight-stitched Xs can be added almost as quickly. Remember to go as far as you can with each line of stitching by thinking "outside the rectangle" (page 33).

(Full quilt, page 36)
Straight-stitched diagonal Xs (marked with tape)
Stitch from the quilt's lower left to the upper right.

30-weight thread

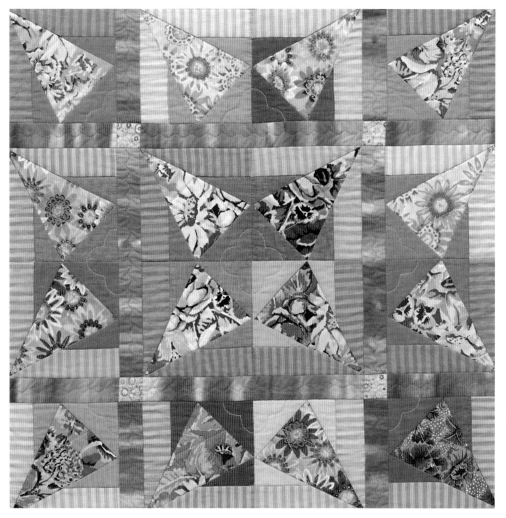

(Full quilt, page 34)
Decorative stitching
Stitch top to bottom and side to side for the length and width of the entire quilt.

40-weight thread

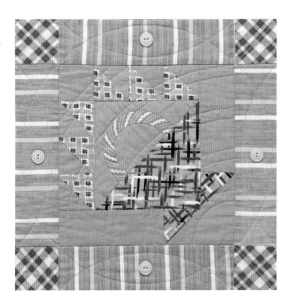

(Full quilt, page 40)
Curved lines (paper-folded and cut)
Stitch from one sashing to another
around the block.
Buttons

30-weight thread

(Full quilt, page 50)
Straight-stitched diagonal lines (marked with tape)

30-weight thread

(Full quilt, page 58)
Curved lines (paper-folded and cut)
Mirror stitching (using edge of walking foot)

30-weight thread

Decorative machine blanket stitching
Mirror stitching of curve
(using edge of walking foot; 40-weight thread)
Rickrack + French knots (30-weight thread)

Harajuku Street Fashion

Bordering Your Quilt

MAKING A PLAN

To many quilters, borders are there simply "because they are." Borders were something quilters learned to do in beginning quiltmaking. They are an afterthought or something to add to make the quilt the right size.

The majority of my quilts have some kind of border treatment. Borders can do any of the following:

- Stop the action or calm the quilt

- Add spark to liven up the quilt

- Reinforce themes in the middle of the quilt by repeating shapes or fabric styles

- Add a sense of completion to a composition

- Provide an opportunity for "something special" piecing

- Showcase wonderful fabrics or pretty quilting

Begin by deciding how much more time you want to invest in your project, as quilted borders can be either very utilitarian, get-the-job-done-in-a-hurry stitching or more luxurious, time-consuming work. It is easier to stitch borders than the quilt center, because they're at the edge of the quilt. Consider challenging yourself. How about a different pattern for each border so you can try more ideas?

GETTING AROUND THE CORNERS

One of the biggest hurdles that stops quilters from quilting interesting borders is the dilemma of how to continue the pattern around four corners.

Straight Lines

A quick and simple quilting solution for borders is to just use straight lines, which turn or crisscross at the corners. Staggering the distance of your lines makes them more interesting. Adding decorative stitching is yet another option worth trying.

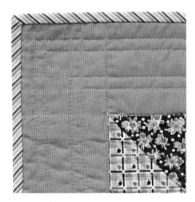

2 rows of straight stitching ¾˝ apart (marked with tape) +
2 more rows of straight stitching (using edge of walking foot)
Rows intersect and cross at the corners.

40-weight thread

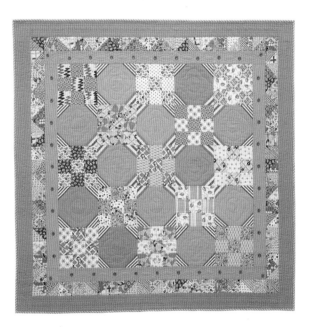

Green Nine-Patch and Snowball

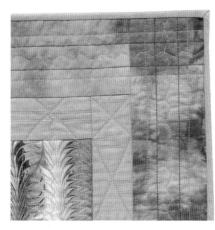

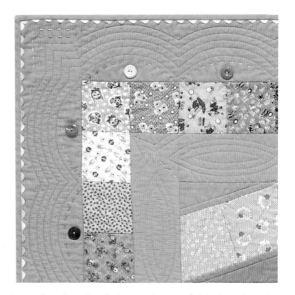

2 rows of straight stitching ¾″ apart (marked with tape) + 2 more rows of straight stitching (using edge of walking foot) + decorative stitching in between
Rows intersect and cross at the corners.

30-weight thread

24-Hour Bliss

Figuring Out a Pattern Turn

I figured out how to take a few of my quilting pattern designs around the corners. It took lots of thought and wasn't easy, but it was worth it.

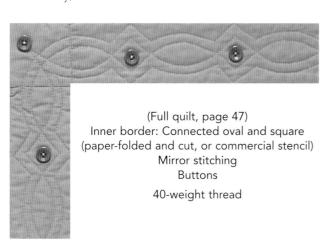

(Full quilt, page 47)
Inner border: Connected oval and square (paper-folded and cut, or commercial stencil)
Mirror stitching
Buttons

40-weight thread

Inner border: Oval shapes (paper-folded and cut)
Mirror stitching (using edge of walking foot; 40-weight thread)

Hand stitching at corners (30-weight thread)
Outer border: Scallop shapes (paper-folded and cut)
Mirror stitching (using edge of walking foot; 40-weight thread)
Hand-stitched variegated Sashiko (30-weight thread)

Corner Blocks

Rather than having to do calculations for corner turns, it's easier to just add fabric corner blocks. These can be stitched in very simple, get-the-job-done stitching with lines or simple motifs. Or you can take a little more time and show off a bit with mirror stitching or compound motifs.

Lines

Stitched X (marked with tape)
30-weight thread

¾˝ + 1˝ stitched grid
(marked with tape)
Buttons
40-weight thread

Follow the lines on a plaid fabric.
40-weight thread

Mirror-curved edge with curved stitching
(using attachable seam guide)
40-weight thread

Motifs

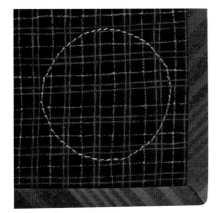

(Full quilt, page 36)
Circle

30-weight thread

(Full quilt, page 36)
Star (traced, drawn, or
commercial template)

30-weight thread

Heart (paper-folded and cut)
Mirror stitching (using inside edge
of walking foot)

30-weight thread

Valentine

Complex Motifs

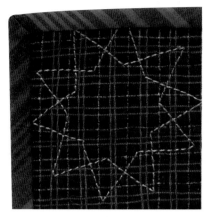

(Full quilt, page 36)
2 stars (traced, drawn, or
commercial template)

30-weight thread

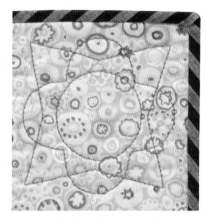

(Full quilt, page 34)
Flower + 4-pointed star
(paper-folded and cut) + circle

30-weight thread

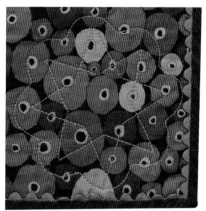

(Full quilt, page 42)
Scalloped flower (commercial
template) + 2 stars (traced, drawn,
or commercial template)

30-weight thread

Flower (paper-folded and cut) + circle

30-weight thread

Green Feed Sack Baskets

ENHANCING THE FABRIC IN BORDERS

Let the fabric print help guide the quilting design for borders.

(Full quilt, page 34)
Straight stitching for lattice
background design

40-weight thread

(Full quilt, page 46)
Follow chain design (40-weight thread) +
hand-stitched circles around flowers (30-weight thread)

(Full quilt, page 51)
Straight stitching (30-weight thread)
+ zigzag stitching (40-weight thread)
on diagonal plaid

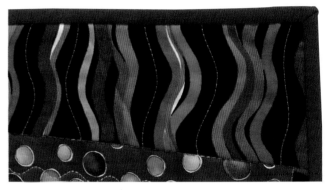

(Full quilt, page 34)
Curvy stitching in slanted, curvy-stripe border fabric

40-weight thread

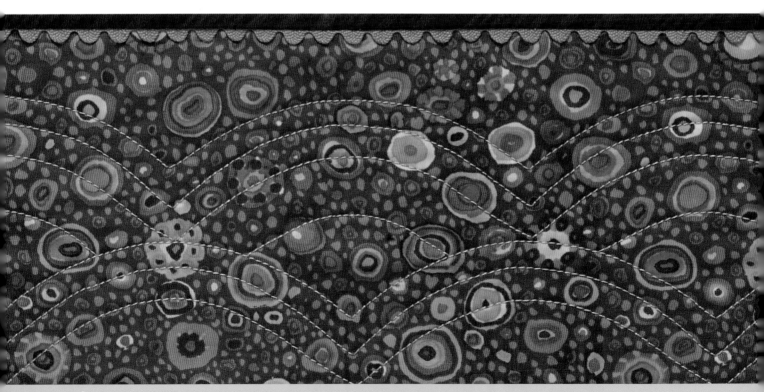

GRID BORDERS

Stitched grids are very successful in quilt borders. Contrasting or heavier threads showcase the stitching best.

To create a diamond or square grid border, sew two lines of stitching, each beginning at one end and stitched to the other end of the border. To mark the grid, use a ruler and mark with pins to evenly divide both sides of your border. Two pieces of tape can be your guide as you stitch from point to point in a zigzag pattern. Keep pivoting and repositioning the tape as you stitch. Start again on the opposite side and complete the grid by connecting the remaining pins.

(Full quilt, page 43)
Straight-stitched diamonds (marked with tape)
40-weight thread

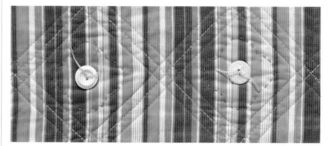

Straight-stitched squares (marked with tape;
30-weight thread) + hand-stitched flower
(paper-folded and cut; 40-weight thread)
Buttons

Create a diamond grid by sewing 2 lines.

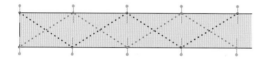

Divide border into equal segments and mark with
pins to create a diamond or square grid.

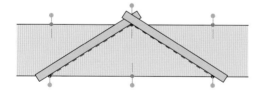

Place tape, from point to point, as a guide. Stitch.

For a more challenging design, I used a commercial stencil template (Basket Weave Stencil from Kitty's Quilt Korner, page 62) to make a curvy-line border grid. I sectioned and marked along the borders in equal segments. From freezer paper, I drew and cut two long, continuous lines for the length of the border and five shorter ones for the width. I concentrated on positioning and stitching one line at a time along my markings. Then, after the grid was stitched, I added decorative stitching.

(Full quilt, page 61)
Curvy lines (commercial stencil) + decorative stitching
30-weight thread

CREATING YOUR OWN BORDER TEMPLATES

Simple connected motifs can be the beginning of wonderful borders. When you're creating your templates, take into consideration the following:

1. Width and length of the borders

2. Size of the blocks in the quilt

3. Whether the blocks are sashed (Sashing will add to your calculations in #2.)

4. Location of the midway or halfway point for possible centering of shapes

5. Whether you already have any shapes on hand that might work

6. Whether you want to tackle something new

In a continuously stitched design, there are only starts and stops at each end of the border, no matter how complicated the stitching looks.

Determining the size of a connected motif border is not an exact science. After considering the points just mentioned, I begin cutting experimental motifs that are anywhere from 6″–10″ in length. When I finally decide on a motif, I trace and cut enough repeats to fill one border from freezer or contact paper.

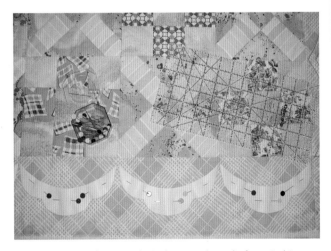

Scallop motifs pinned in place and ready for stitching

Curved Scallop Borders

To create scallops, you can paper-cut your first curve or draw it with a ruler made specifically for making curves (such as Katie's Scallop Radial Rule, page 62). You will need enough templates to quilt the length of one border. Sometimes it's necessary to also have partial pieces for beginning and ending centered designs.

Try adding mirror stitching. Use the edge of the walking foot or an attachable seam guide if you have one. You can add more or fewer rows depending on the look you want.

Also try staggering your rows. To do so, you will need to locate midpoints and have half-templates (see Positioning and Stitching Around Templates, page 30).

(Full quilt, page 36)
Straight stitching (marked with tape) + curves
(paper-folded and cut, or curved ruler)
Mirror stitching
Buttons
30-weight thread

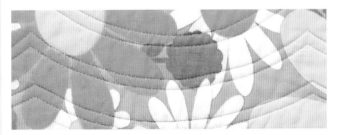

Curves (paper-folded and cut,
or curved ruler)
1″ mirror stitching
(attachable seam guide and
edge of walking foot)
40-weight thread

Out of Sight Circles

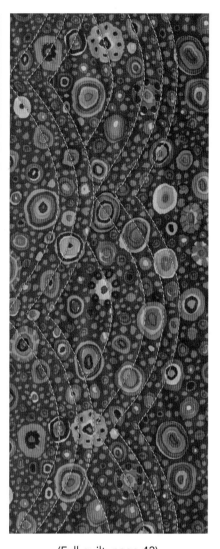

(Full quilt, page 42)
Curves (paper-folded and cut, or
curved ruler) + 2 rows mirror stitching
of curves + one smaller inside curve
(attachable seam guide)

30-weight thread

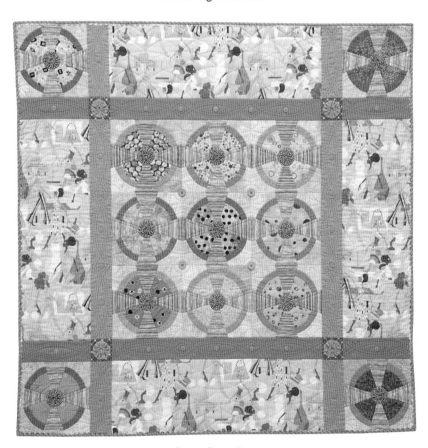

Serendipity Dots

Curves (paper-folded and cut, or
curved ruler) +
midpoint staggering of next row

40-weight thread

Serpentine-Stitched Cable Borders

The easiest way to stitch a border is to stitch two lines, each going from the beginning to the end of the border. Pointed oval templates are used to make cables. Position the oval templates and then serpentine stitch from side to side as you continue down around the line of ovals. It is easier to keep going on a soft curve of stitching than to pivot and stay on the same side of the ovals. Just leave a little room between the ovals to stitch through the intersections.

Line 1   Line 2

Stitch pointed ovals in serpentine pattern to create cable.

Simple Cables

The first cable below has been left unadorned so that you can see the simple connected shapes. The other three cables all look different because each was stitched differently after the initial serpentine stitching around the ovals. For each, I started on the outsides of the first oval and used 30-weight thread.

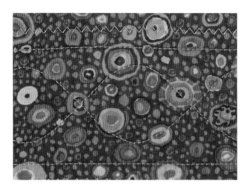

(Full quilt, page 42)
Ovals (paper-folded and cut) +
straight stitching
(marked with tape) +
decorative stitching

Ovals (paper-folded and cut)
Mirror stitching on left and right sides of oval row
Pivot at intersections and stay on the same side
to achieve cables of all the same size.

Ovals (paper-folded and cut)
Serpentine mirror stitching outside the first oval leads to the inside
of the second oval to achieve large and small cables

Ovals (paper-folded and cut)
Stitch inside and outside all ovals to achieve cables all the same size.

Complex Cables

Once the concept of serpentine stitched cables is understood, the fun begins. Additional lines and lines using decorative stitches can be added. Most machines have zigzag and two-step zigzag stitches (for knits). Bernina machines have a serpentine stitch. Remember to elongate and/or widen the stitches. Experiment.

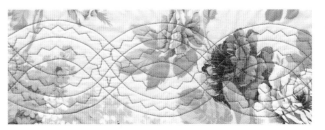

Cable (paper-folded and cut)
+ decorative stitching added to both sides

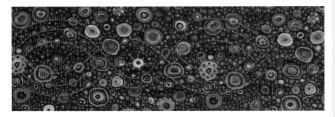

(Full quilt, page 42)
Alternating large and small ovals (paper-folded and cut)
+ pivoted mirror stitching
+ additional inner lines around larger ovals

Cable (paper-folded and cut)
+ decorative stitching added to both sides
+ additional straight and mirror stitching

Flower Garden

Pivoted Cables

The first cable I ever stitched was a small pivoted cable in which ovals and squares were combined. I used a commercial quilting stencil and made freezer-paper templates for a small inner border.

Serpentine stitch the ovals and squares together like simple cables. But in this case, stop, pivot, and reposition on the outside corners of the squares as you change direction. Additional mirror stitching fills up the border and makes the cable look more complex. You won't be able to use decorative stitching, however, as that only works on soft curves.

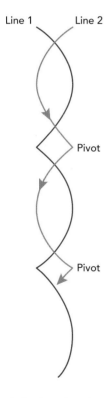

Serpentine-stitched oval and square cables:
It's necessary to stop and pivot on the square.

Oval and square cable (paper-folded and cut)
+ 2 rows of mirror serpentine stitching (using edge of walking foot) beginning on outside of square

30-weight thread

Bugs Quilt

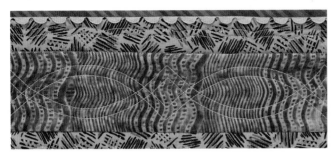

Oval and square cable (paper-folded and cut)
Same as previous cable but different proportions
Additional narrow border strips with decorative scallop
stitch + mirror stitching (using edge of walking foot)

30-weight thread

(Full quilt, page 50)
Oval and square cable (paper-folded and cut) + serpentine
mirror stitching (using edge of walking foot) on both sides
of original stitching

30-weight thread

(Full quilt, page 36)
Oval and square (paper-folded and cut)
Mirror stitching on inside of ovals only (using edge of walking foot)

30-weight thread

New Zealand Quilt

SWAG BORDERS

I have always loved appliquéd swag borders, but they didn't seem quite right for me or for any of my quilts. Recently, however, I viewed a swag border quilt with new eyes. It dawned on me that I could quilt the swags rather than appliqué them!

To challenge myself even more, I decided I needed four different swag designs. Because the pieced blocks were unsashed, I considered the block size and the border width when selecting the size rectangles to fold in half and paper-cut. I left room for some mirror stitching. The borders became progressively more challenging to stitch as I moved around each side of the quilt. I used 30-weight thread.

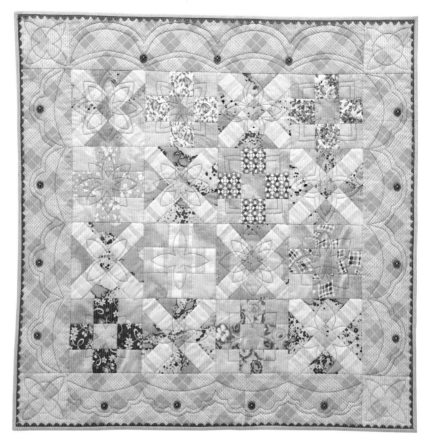

Adrian's Challenge

Swags (paper-folded and cut)
Mirror stitching on top and bottom edges
(using edge of walking foot)
Buttons

Swags (paper-folded and cut)
Mirror stitching (using edge of walking foot)
on bottom of 3-curve swags
Buttons

Swags (paper-folded and cut)
Mirror stitching (using edge of walking foot)
on bottom of 3-curve swags
Buttons

Swags (paper-folded and cut)
Mirror stitching (using edge of walking foot)
on bottom of 5-curve swags
Buttons

BAPTIST FAN BORDERS

The Baptist Fan design is a traditional allover quilting pattern that I have learned to use in different ways. I first used it for a French reproduction fabric border that was too gorgeous to just quilt with straight lines. I laid my Baptist Fan templates on the fabric and had an "a-ha" moment. I could stitch quilted patterns over printed fabrics!

Five years later, when I was searching for what to do with another busy floral, I used the Baptist Fan again. However, I went even further with additions I've since learned to do. I used 30-weight thread.

(Full quilt, page 20)
Baptist Fan arcs
(commercial quilting stencil)

Baptist Fan arcs (commercial quilting stencil)

Baptist Fan arcs (commercial quilting stencil) + decorative stitching
(using edge of walking foot)

Baptist Fan arcs (commercial quilting stencil) + flower commercial template
+ 2 circles + decorative hand stitching

CONCLUSION

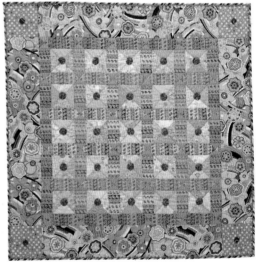

Summer of Love

My mother was a teacher. One of her goals was to learn something new each day. Learning never really ends, no matter how skilled we become. Challenging myself to quilt each top in a different way has stretched my creativity. I've learned a lot. By concentrating on what I could do rather than what I couldn't, I've found that there is a tremendous amount that can be done with a great machine, good walking foot, wonderful supplies, an avid imagination, and tons of practice. I already have new designs buzzing in my head.

Resources

Stencils, Templates, Rulers

JUNE TAILOR
www.junetailor.com
Template sets: flower, circle, star
Nested, but can only use larger size

KATIE LANE QUILTS
www.katielane.com
Scallop Radial Rules: 6″–10″ and 2″–5″
Two arc scallops for each inch increment

KITTY'S QUILT KORNER
64 Standard Street
Newington, CT 06111
(860) 666-4414
EL14 Basket Weave template

QUILTER'S RULE
www.quiltersrule.com
(800) 343-8671
Template sets: daisy, circle, diamond, oval
Nested, but can only use larger size

THE STENCIL COMPANY
28 Castlewood Drive, Dept. C
Cheektowaga, NY 14227-2615
www.quiltingstencils.com
info@quiltingstencils.com

Baptist Fan quilting stencils (also called Bishops, Amish, or Methodist Fan)

Many other shapes, but look at silhouettes. For example, some flowers will give a scallop flower shape.

Threads

AURIFIL COTTON MAKO 12 THREAD
That Thread Shop
(708) 301-3172
www.allthatthread.com

YLI CORPORATION JEANS STITCH
(803) 985-3100
www.ylicorp.com (Use retail store locator.)

Ergonomic Tilt Table and Footrest

SEW-ERGO
(888) 739-8458
www.sew-ergo.com

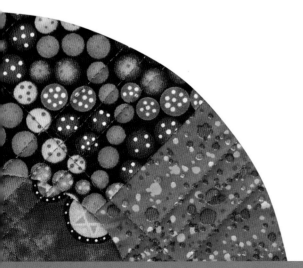

About the Author

Mary Mashuta began quilting in the early 1970s and has been teaching quiltmaking internationally since 1985. Her quilts and garments have been in numerous national shows.

Mary began as a hand quilter, but she switched to machine quilting with the walking foot in the 1990s. She prides herself on creating interesting quilting designs with the walking foot and has discovered how to use heavier threads on the top of the machine. Because she never moved on to free-motion quilting, she has been able to help numerous other quilters who are "drop the feed dog" challenged to discover that they can quilt their own quilts with interesting designs without ever doing free-motion quilting.

Mary has two degrees in home economics. This is her sixth book for C&T. She has also written numerous magazine articles. She lives in Berkeley, California, with her sister and fellow quilter, Roberta Horton. Visit Mary at www.marymashuta.com.

Great Titles from

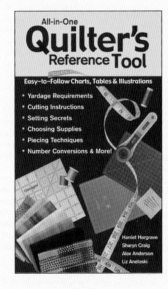